THE BIG SIX

US AIRLINES

GEOFF JONES

Airlife
England

Copyright © 2000 Geoffrey P. Jones

First published in the UK in 2000
by Airlife Publishing Ltd

British Library Cataloguing-in-Publication Data
A catalogue record for this book
is available from the British Library

ISBN 1 84037 176 5

Typeset by Rowland Phototypesetting Ltd, Bury St Edmunds,
Suffolk.
Printed in China.

Airlife Publishing Ltd
101 Longden Road, Shrewsbury, SY3 9EB, England
E-mail: airlife@airlifebooks.com
Website: www.airlifebooks.com

Front Cover Pictures
Top left: Northwest Airbus A320 at San Francisco.
Top right: Delta Boeing 767-232 *Spirit of Delta* purchased by Delta employees during a financial crisis
                 in 1982/83.
Middle left: Continental Airlines activity at Houston George Bush Intercontinental, the airline's main hub.
Middle right: One of US Airways' fleet of forty Fokker F100s at push-back at its Charlotte, N.C. hub.
Bottom left: American Airlines Boeing 727, one of over 70 of the type still in service.
Bottom right: United Airlines was launch customer for the huge Boeing 777 twin-jet.

Contents

Back Cover Pictures

Top left: Continental tails, Boeing 777 nearest, and DC-10-30 beyond, at London (Gatwick) from where they now fly six daily services to the US.

Right: Northwest's transatlantic services to London (Gatwick), previously flown by Boeing 747-200s, are now flown by DC-10s, this pair seen at the satellite of the south terminal in July 1999.

Bottom left: Charlotte during a US Airways traffic 'bank'. The airport handles over 23 million passengers a year, 95% of them on US Airways. Charlotte is ranked twentieth in the US in terms of total passengers but fifth in terms of hubs.

Introduction

This book details and describes in words and pictures six huge US-based airlines: American Airlines, United Airlines, Delta Air Lines, Northwest Airlines, US Airways and Continental Airlines – some of the world's largest airlines. The definition of why these are the 'Big Six', the six largest airlines based in the USA, is simply in terms of traffic. This is measured in revenue passenger kilometres or RPKs. There are also major historic reasons for classifying these airlines as being at the top of the tree – their histories can all be traced back to the 1920s and 1930s and they were often the carriers of airmail on the formative US airmail routes. Since the demise of the Soviet Union and its all-embracing airline, Aeroflot – although this still survives as Russia's international airline, but is now much smaller – these six US airlines are amongst the world's largest airlines.

Some other airlines, such as Trans World Airlines (TWA) and Southwest Airlines, come close to joining the 'Big Six', but fail in the case of TWA because it just does not match up in terms of size, RPKs and passengers carried. Southwest, whilst knocking at the door for entry to this classification, is none the less just outside in the numbers game, and in any case does not have the historical and international pedigree that set these 'Big Six' apart from their current near rivals.

However, if different criteria to RPKs are applied, such as passenger numbers, then those in this 'Big Six' category change slightly, as can be seen from the following tabulation of data for the four years 1996 to 1999 inclusive:

The fickle nature of the US air transport industry and its susceptibility to change and outside effects is legendary. In 1978 the US Congress passed the Deregulation Act, generally accepted as a watershed in the current US air transport industry. If this book had been prepared in the 1970s, the airlines featuring as part of the 'Big Six' would have been entirely different from those currently featured. In 1978 American Airlines' fleet numbered 269 aircraft and Delta's 209 aircraft. In contrast Northwest Orient Airlines had a fleet of only 109 aircraft and Continental a mere 67 aircraft. However, Eastern Air Lines' fleet was almost as large as American's at 235 aircraft, TWA's fleet numbered 248 aircraft and PanAm's 103 aircraft. United Airlines though was probably the largest US-based airline, if fleet size is the criteria, with 409 aircraft, although at this time its route network was entirely domestic plus services to Honolulu. Readers will need no reminder that Eastern no longer exists and that PanAm, a very small charter airline in 1999, does not merit any comment other than the continuance of this historic name.

Some of the small and medium-sized US-based airlines flying in 1978 are an interesting record of the time and the subsequent, dramatic changes there have been in this industry:

Air California (AirCal) (was taken over by American Airlines)
Air Florida (came and went)
Alaska Airlines (a small, twelve-aircraft fleet, grew steadily

Airline	Traffic (RPK in millions)				Passenger numbers (million)			
	1999	1998	1997	1996	1999	1998	1997	1996
United Airlines	202,000	200,606	195,408	187,765	87.16	87	84.48	86.00
American Airlines	180,428	175,217	172,203	168,478	84.75	81	80.70	79.30
Delta Air Lines	168,701	166,271	160,400	151,130	105.53	105	102.90	97.28
Northwest Airlines	119,410	107,382	115,901	110,440	56.11	50	54.12	32.70
Continental Airlines	96,635	86,741	77,082	67,440	45.54	44	41.56	35.64
US Airways	66,916	66,565	67,176	62,659	55.81	58	58.67	79.32

In 1999, in terms of the total number of passengers carried, Dallas (Love Field)-based low-fare carrier Southwest Airlines carried 57.5 million passengers, more than US Airways, Northwest and Continental. Again though, because of Southwest's entirely domestic and short–medium haul route network and because its traffic RPK was 58,731, lower than all those of the 'Big Six', it fails. If this book were being written next year, there is no reason why Southwest may not have made the grade in terms of RPKs.

and now carries over thirteen million passengers annually)
Allegheny Airlines (became USAir and in 1997 US Airways)
Braniff International Airways (grew rapidly but failed)
Frontier Airlines (Denver-based regional carrier taken over by Continental in 1986)
Hughes Airwest (Californian carrier merged with Republic in 1980)
National Airlines (rapidly growing national and

international carrier taken over by PanAm)

North Central Airlines (became Republic Airlines when merged with Southern Airways, and then subsequently Northwest Airlines)

Ozark Air Lines (merged with TWA)

Pacific Southwest Airlines (merged with USAir and then became US Airways)

Piedmont Airlines (merged with USAir and then became US Airways)

Southern Airways (see above – merged with Republic and then became part of Northwest)

Southwest Airlines (fleet of sixteen Boeing 737s, had started schedules on 18 June 1971)

Texas International (became embroiled in the Eastern Air Lines survival/failure story)

Western Airlines (taken over by Delta in 1987)

The mid-1970s were also the time that small commuter airlines started to spring up all over the US, feeding local traffic with small commuter-type aircraft into larger airports, the start of practical hub-and-spoke operations. Allegheny Airlines pioneered this type of operation and in 1967 Henson Airlines was established as the first Allegheny Commuter airline. The profusion of smaller express-style airlines, wearing the identity and liveries of their bigger associates are now an integral part of the US air transport scene, an important feature of the operations of all of the 'Big Six' airlines, and are profusely illustrated in this book. However, many of these express-type operators, whilst associated with the 'Big Six', are not owned by the airline in whose livery they appear. They use the big brother's identity on a franchising basis, but remain independent. There can be no generalisations though; three of US Airways' Express operators (Allegheny, Piedmont and PSA) being wholly owned subsidiaries. Similarly Continental Express is also a wholly owned subsidiary. There are many variations within these Express operations – Northwest Airlines has acquired RJ 85s on behalf of its Northwest Airlink operator, Mesaba Airlines. Some Express operators fly on behalf of more than one airline in the 'Big Six', Skywest Airlines having alliances with both Delta and United, for instance, and Gulfstream International Airlines with Continental and United. Commuter-type airlines also switch allegiance, such as Colgan Air's move in late 1999 from being a Continental Connection carrier to a US Airways Express carrier.

Variations in equipment are also notable amongst the associate express operators of the 'Big Six'. Whilst many are happy to utilise turbo-props such as the ATR-42, ATR-72, Raytheon B1900, DHC-8 and Embraer EMB-120 Brasilia, some are switching wholesale to the burgeoning regional-jet market. Continental Express, for instance, stated in 1998 that in five years it would phase out its entire turbo-prop fleet and move to an all-jet fleet (Embraer ERJ-145 and 135s). In late 1999 AMR Eagle, who operates American Airlines' American Eagle express/commuter airline, announced that, although it operates the world's largest fleet of turbo-prop Saab 340s (115 aircraft), it was now phasing these out. Their replacements are to be turbofan-powered Embraer ERJ-135s and ERJ-145s, and possibly the newly announced forty-four-seat ERJ-140. Similarly American Eagle will also replace its thirty- eight ATR-72s with seventy-seat Bombardier CRJ-700s from 2001 onwards.

In an unusual twist to the operations of these 'Express-type' airlines, Northwest Airlines announced in March 2000 that it was to code-share on American Eagle Saab 340B services at Los Angeles. Links between Northwest and AA have never previously occurred, at least not publicly. From 18 March this code-share will operate on flights to seven American Eagle destinations in California.

The magnitudes of these 'Big Six' can also be identified in the total number of their employees, statistics quoted being from late 1999:

American Airlines	–	100,951
United Airlines	–	100,000
Delta Air Lines	–	65,000
Northwest Airlines	–	52,000
US Airways	–	43,028
Continental Airlines	–	49,300

Southwest Airlines has only 26,949 employees and TWA 25,000, another measure of inclusion or non-inclusion in the 'Big Six'. Profitability has not always been a byword with these airlines, although in recent years, with a few exceptions, the booming US economy has enabled most of the 'Big Six' to report substantial profits. The days of filing for Chapter 11 bankruptcy protection are not that far away though, Continental having the ignominy of having to file twice, in September 1983 and 1991, and Northwest in 1989.

The US air transport industry is responsible for the carriage of huge numbers of passengers (1,314 million in North America in 1998) and huge amounts of freight as well (28,889,317 metric tonnes in North America in 1998). The top ten US airlines carried 550 million intra and extra passengers in 1999, 3% up on 1998.

There is no sizeable town or city that does not have a scheduled air service by one of the 'Big Six' or one of its associate or affiliate airlines. The only possible exceptions within the fifty-one United States are the Hawaiian chain of islands in the Pacific and Alaska. Because of their geographical circumstances the Hawaiian Islands are served from the US mainland by some of the 'Big Six', but Aloha Airlines and Hawaiian Airlines fly the majority of the inter-island services. Aloha has an alliance with United and Hawaiian has alliances with American, Continental (plus Continental Micronesia) and Northwest. In Alaska several of the 'Big Six' serve the main population centres of Fairbanks and Anchorage, but because of the geographical and climatological peculiarities of the State, highly specialist local airlines provide the feed for passengers and cargo to and from the two main cities.

All six of the 'Big Six' airlines have international services from the US to the UK (and European destinations), mainly to London's Heathrow and Gatwick airports, but to an increasing extent to Manchester. In September 1999 US Airways announced that it hoped to start a new daily, non-stop Philadelphia to Manchester service in the spring of 2000. Continental is already well established at Manchester, Birmingham and Glasgow. The appearance of these airlines in Europe has largely resulted from the demise of the traditional US scheduled transatlantic carrier

PanAm and the inroads made by these carriers into the services of survivor TWA.

Delta Air Lines was one of the first of the current 'Big Six' to fly transatlantic schedules, commencing Atlanta to London (Gatwick) services in April 1978 using Lockheed L1011 Tristars. Delta had previously flown transatlantic charters to Europe between 1969 and 1973 using ex-PanAm DC-8-33s. One of the other newcomers on transatlantic services was Northwest Airlines – during the phase when it was named Northwest Orient Airlines – first commencing cargo flights from Boston and New York to Glasgow in February 1979, followed by their first passenger flights to Glasgow in April and to London (Gatwick) in June. Northwest, like Delta, has had a continuous and strong presence on the North Atlantic and at Gatwick ever since. US charter airlines and up-and-coming scheduled airlines also competed vigorously for transatlantic passengers at this time – airlines such as Braniff, World, Capitol International, Western, Air Florida and People Express. In contrast, American Airlines, although it had temporarily flown the North Atlantic between 1945 and 1950, did not start scheduled services from the US to Europe until its new Boeing 767-200ERs had been certificated for such flights in 1982. Again American's UK terminal was London (Gatwick), BA, PanAm and TWA maintaining their stranglehold on London (Heathrow). United Airlines was even later in breaking out from homeland US, not commencing international flights until April 1983 between the Pacific Northwest of the US and Tokyo. Services from the US to Europe by United did not commence until 1988. Continental started its first true international service (not including services to Canada and Mexico) in May 1979. They flew Los Angeles to New Zealand and Australia via Honolulu and US Samoa. It was not until the unsavoury Frank Lorenzo takeover of Continental by the Texas Air Corporation and Eastern Air Lines, followed quickly by New York Air and People Express, that Continental and its new International Division started services to London in 1987. One of US Airways' predecessors, Charlotte, North Carolina-based Piedmont Airlines was claimed to be the fastest-expanding US airline during the mid-1980s. An indicator of this expansion was Piedmont's order for Boeing 767-200ERs and the start of its daily Charlotte–London (Gatwick) scheduled services in June 1987.

Passenger air transport in North America (note not the US) in 1998 represented the carriage of a total of 1,314,883,795 passengers, a 2.2% increase on 1997. The carriage of these passengers, and twenty-eight million tonnes of freight, required a total of 31,874,731 aircraft movements. A significant proportion of these aircraft movements were recorded at the airlines' hubs – hub-and-spoke operations are the model for the whole air transport industry. It is largely the geographical vastness of the USA and the availability of more affordable air travel that have helped these hubs to develop and prosper. The hub airports are merely air transport 'crossroads' or the 1990s' equivalents of the big English railway junctions such as Crewe and Clapham Junction of an earlier era.

Indicative of a typical US hub airport is Charlotte in North Carolina, where US Airways are the dominant carrier, responsible for 95% of the twenty-three million passengers that currently use the airport annually. Of this 95% only 20% of passengers actually originate locally in the Charlotte area (or 'come through the front door'); 80% of US Airways passengers using Charlotte are just 'hubbing it', connecting there from one flight to another. The main US hub airports of the 'Big Six' are as follows – some of these airlines have established hubs at international locations, most notably Northwest who have strong Japanese hubs at Tokyo (Narita) and Osaka (Kansai):

American – Chicago (O'Hare), Dallas/Fort Worth, Miami, San Juan (Luis Munoz Marin) Puerto Rico
United – Chicago (O'Hare), Denver, San Francisco, Washington (Dulles) International
Delta – Atlanta Hartsfield (Worldport), Cincinnati/North Kentucky International, Dallas/Fort Worth, Salt Lake City, New York (John F. Kennedy)
Northwest – Minneapolis/St Paul (Twin Cities), Detroit, Memphis
Continental – Houston (George Bush Intercontinental), Newark (New York), Cleveland-Hopkins International
US Airways – Pittsburgh (International), Charlotte (Douglas) International, Philadelphia International, Baltimore/Washington International

Largest of the 'Big Six' in terms of number of passengers carried annually is currently Delta Air Lines, exceeding its nearest rival United by over eighteen million. This magnitude is now reflected in the rankings of the biggest airports (by passenger traffic) in the US. Chicago O'Hare (a major hub for United and American), quoted for many years as 'the biggest', has now been toppled from the *number one* position by Delta's main operational base and main hub, Atlanta Hartsfield in Georgia, now known as Atlanta Worldport.

Top US Airports by Passenger Traffic/ Major Multi-Airport Systems 1998

Airport	Passengers*	% change from 1997
ATLANTA (ATL)	73,474,298	+ 7.7
CHICAGO (ORD)	72,369,951	+ 3.0
LOS ANGELES (LAX)	61,216,072	+ 1.8
DALLAS/FT.WORTH (DFW)	60,482,700	+/- 0.0
SAN FRANCISCO (SFO)	40,059,975	- 1.1
DENVER (DEN)	36,817520	+5.3
NEW YORK (Newark)	(est) 32,445,000	+5.0
NEW YORK (JFK)	(est) 31,295,000	- 0.2
LAS VEGAS (McCarran)	30,217,665	- 0.3

* Total passengers enplaned and deplaned; passengers in transit count once.

If one then looks at these and other US airports in terms of aircraft movements in 1998 (defined as landing and take-off of an aircraft) then slightly different rankings appear:

Top Ten US Airports by Aircraft Movements/ Major Multi-Airport Systems 1998

Airport	Movements	% change from '97 if available
CHICAGO (ORD)	897,354	+ 1.7
ATLANTA (ATL)	846,881	—
DALLAS/FT.WORTH	836,079	—
LOS ANGELES (LAX)	773,569	- 1.3
DETROIT (DTW)	542,440	—
PHOENIX (PHX)	537,822	—
MIAMI (MIA)	536,262	—
BOSTON (BOS)	507,449	—
OAKLAND (California) (OAK)	506,628	—
ST LOUIS (STL)	503,736	—

(Statistical data from Airports Council International (ACI))

Air cargo has already been identified as an important element of the US air transport industry, and whilst all the 'Big Six' carry huge amounts of air cargo annually, some of them are more dedicated to this element of air transport than others. Northwest, for instance, has a dedicated air cargo subsidiary, currently with nine 100%-dedicated Boeing 747-200F freighters. United has four dedicated DC-10-30Fs, but expects to phase these out of service as the few remaining passenger DC-10s in its fleet are retired by 2001 – if a Boeing 777 freighter were available, United have said they would be interested in this as a replacement. Dedicated cargo airlines outside of the 'Big Six' account for much of the cargo volume and for the rankings of those US airports handling the most air cargo. Memphis, for instance, is the Federal Express cargo hub and Louisville United Parcel Service's cargo hub.

Top US Airports by Cargo Volume 1998

Airport	Tonnes*	% change from '97
MEMPHIS (MEM)	2,368,973	+ 6.1
LOS ANGELES (LAX)	1,861,049	- 0.7
MIAMI (MIA)	1,793,015	+ 1.5
NEW YORK (JFK)	1,605,300	- 3.7
CHICAGO (ORD)	1,440,033	+ 2.3
LOUISVILLE (SDF)	1,394,999	+ 3.7

*(loaded/unloaded freight + mail)

A growing phenomenon in the US air transport industry and inherent within airlines of the 'Big Six', is the creation of low-fare or low-cost units or airlines within airlines. United created Shuttle by United (officially named United Shuttle) primarily in the western US states, Delta formed Delta Express and most recently in June 1998 US Airways started its MetroJet operation. Most of these have been established to counter the effects – and threats to traffic – of other low-fare airlines, most notably Southwest Airlines. Continental was the pioneer amongst the 'Big Six'. It established CALite for largely short-haul services and revived its earlier 'peanuts fares' in 1993, targeting mainly the eastern Piedmont region and Florida and then expanding into New England. However, its existence was short-lived, although by the summer of 1994 CALite was flying 167 daily CALite flights with a dedicated fleet of Boeing 737 and DC-9 aircraft. Increased competition, low yields and the need to concentrate on more established core activities saw the demise of CALite after two years. The low-fare units of 'Big Six' airlines, United's Shuttle by United, Delta's Delta Express and US Airways MetroJet, have all used the same aircraft to initiate their operations, the Boeing 737-200. These have been drawn from the airlines' mainline fleets, reconfigured in one-class layouts and re-identified with the new operational name and livery. More recently Shuttle by United have introduced newer Boeing 737-300 and 737-500s to replace the older, less economic 737-200s. Delta and US Airways' low-fare operations have been primarily targeted at consumers in the eastern seaboard region of the US and in particular the Florida vacation and holiday markets.

Airline alliances have been one of the biggest vogue trends in recent years. Setting the standard, which has not yet been equalled, has been the alliance between Northwest Airlines and Dutch airline KLM. In January 1993 the two airlines were granted anti-trust immunity by the US Department of Transportation. This enabled these two airlines to operate their transatlantic flights as a joint-venture alliance in relation to pricing, scheduling, product development and marketing. This was beyond the usual and more common airline alliance, generally just a code-share agreement. The Northwest/KLM alliance has increased what might have been a moderate 5% per annum growth in traffic to a phenomenal 15%. The widely publicised proposed alliance between American Airlines and British Airways has still not achieved consummation, and seems unlikely to develop beyond the level of the two airlines grouping within the **one**world alliance. The US Department of Transportation dismissed the application from the airlines for anti-trust immunity. The US government has also taken the lead in sanctioning the deeper alliance trend that some of the 'Big Six' seek. Other government entities, particularly the European Commission, have been more concerned over the potential impact on competition and the perceived threat of US airlines dominating the marketplace.

Nonetheless, alliances in various 'depths' are now very much a fact of airline life, code-shares between US and foreign carriers numbering 163 in mid-1999, compared to only sixty-one in 1994. And whilst some airlines may look enviously at Northwest and KLM's foresight (and luck?) in securing their anti-trust immunity when they did, the alliance is here to stay as part of the globalisation of the airline industry. The main alliances currently in force with those airlines of the 'Big Six' are as follows:

AIRLINE ALLIANCES (believed correct at Feb 2000)

	Current	Pending
American Airlines (oneworld)	British Airways	Aer Lingus
	Qantas	Japan Air Lines
	Cathay Pacific	LanChile
	Canadian Airlines	
	Iberia	
	Finnair	

(Continued on page 10)

AIRLINE ALLIANCES *(continued)*

	Current	Pending
United Airlines (Star Alliance)	Lufthansa	British Midland
	SAS Scandinavian	Canadian Airlines
	Thai Airways	Austrian Airlines
	Air Canada	Lauda Air
	Varig	Tyrolean Airways
	All Nippon Airways	Mexicana
	Ansett Australia	
	Singapore Airlines	
Delta Air Lines	Air France	AeroMexico
		Korean Air
Northwest Airlines (Wings)	KLM	Kenya Airways
Continental	Alitalia	Braathens
		Air Europa
US Airways	American Airlines (marketing alliance only)	Olympic

NB the fifth big alliance is the **Qualifier Group** which currently does not have one of the BIG SIX airlines as a member. For completeness the current members of Qualifier are:
Swissair, Crossair, SABENA, Austrian Airlines, Lauda Air, Tyrolean Airways, TAP Portugal, Turkish Airlines and AOM. Applications pending for Qualifier are: South African Airways, LOT Polish

One negative reaction to the growth in airline alliances and code-shares has come from the US Federal Aviation Administration (FAA). Their concern is the safety standards of non-US code-share partners. This started with those airlines contracted under the CRAF scheme (Civil Reserve Air Fleet) and those that regularly carry US military personnel. These airlines have all agreed to carry out safety and operational reviews of their foreign marketing partners. It is likely that all partners will be required to carry out similar reviews. The concern has gone as far as to delay code-sharing, American's proposed code-share with China Airlines and Delta's with Korean Air having been put on hold in 1999.

Profitability is what successful airline operations are all about. Most of the 'Big Six' returned positive results in 1999, cumulatively an average net profit of $726 million. However, these airlines' operating margins (profit measured against turnover) fell in 1999 against similar figures in 1998. This was despite the increase in each airline's turnover. Operational performance has therefore declined and although the air transport market they serve has grown, the yields have declined. The low-fare airline competition is one reason, competition which will doubtless affect the 'Big Six' even more in subsequent years.

It is a reasonable bet that, if this book were written in the year 2010, these six airlines would still exist in name and be in at least the US 'top ten'. The 1998-proposed mergers of the mega carriers seemed unlikely, with the 'Big Six' airlines retaining their identities. However, following the May 2000 announcement that United Airlines were to acquire US Airways and become the world's largest airline, is part of the process of consolidation and 'sizing-up'. This merger will put United well ahead of American and Delta, its two closest rivals, in terms of fleet size, RPKs, employees, hubs, routes and of course revenue and hopefully profits. Everything is now in the melting pot and with United paying a staggering $11.6 billion for US Airways, the cost is not perceptibly a major issue.

There will be an effect on air services as a result of alliances because airports will not attract service from an airline whose alliance partner already serves that airport. This is already affecting the directions of capital expenditure on terminal developments and improvements at some of the big US international airports. However, alliances and code-share agreements will not be static. The autumn 1999 withdrawal of Austrian Airlines from the SAir (Swissair) Group-led Qualifier Group (Delta is a SAir Group partner and announced its alliance with Air France, perceived as a major competitor to Swissair) to the United/Lufthansa-led Star Alliance is indicative of this instability. This move also precipitated the collapse of the Atlantic Excellence Alliance. Swissair's proposed code-share deal with Thai Airways also casts doubt over Thai's continuing membership of the Star Alliance.

The commitment of Singapore Airlines to the Star Alliance has also been questioned, particularly with its early 2000 equity purchase of Virgin, and this airline's reluctance to join Star. The development of the hub system in the US will undoubtedly continue to grow and flourish, led largely by the airlines of the 'Big Six' described in this book. As fares remain competitive, leisure travel will grow whilst the requirement for business travel, due to the growth of e-commerce, could well take a dip. Regardless, these 'Big Six' airlines will continue to dominate the deregulated US air transport industry, at least in terms of brand names if not necessarily in terms of ownership, both at home in the United States of America and also globally.

Geoff Jones,
Guernsey, C.I.

American Airlines

The Robertson Aircraft Corporation was founded in Missouri in 1921. It successfully tendered for one of the first Contract Air Mail routes (CAM), which were being awarded to private airline operators under the 1925 Kelly Act. The airline's first CAM operation was flown between St Louis and Chicago flown on 15 April 1926 using a DH 4 biplane piloted by the then unknown Charles Lindbergh. In 1923 Naugatuck, Connecticut-based Bee Line started operations as an aircraft charter company. On 1 July 1926 it flew its first scheduled CAM flight between Boston, Hartford and New York. Passengers were flown by Bee Line for the first time in April 1927. Bee Line became known as Colonial Airways.

In 1929 a holding company, known as the Aviation Corporation, sought to buy up many of the smaller embryo aviation businesses and CAM operators in an attempt to make them a viable trading company. Five principal companies constituted the Aviation Corporation: Colonial Airways, Interstate Air Lines, Inc., Universal Air Lines System, the Embry-Riddle Company and Southern Air Transport. Their diverse interests and assets were finally merged in 1930 as American Airways Inc. New Curtiss Condors were ordered in 1933, the year that the airline's name changed to American Airlines (AA). Soon after, AA ordered the new DC-2 and in 1936 AA took delivery of its first Douglas DC-3 and flew its first commercial flight with the aircraft on 25 June between Chicago and New York.

Freight operations with DC-3s, DC-4s and then DC-6s during World War II and immediately after helped establish AA and in 1947 it inaugurated the first transcontinental sleeper flights using DC-6s flying from New York to Los Angeles via Chicago. Its last DC-3 was retired from service in 1949. Non-stop transcontinental flights were inaugurated by AA in 1953 using DC-7s. In 1959 AA introduced the airline's first turbo-prop, the Lockheed Electra, complemented in the same year on its transcontinental service by its first jet, the Boeing 707. The airline introduced Convair 990s in 1961 and its first Boeing 727 in 1964. Its last DC-6 flew its final service with AA on 17 December 1966. Wide-body Boeing 747s and then Douglas DC-10s joined the AA fleet in 1970 and 1971 respectively.

In June 1975 AA swapped its trans-Pacific routes with PanAm for their Caribbean authority (Jamaica, Guadeloupe and Martinique) – and Montreal, Canada – reinforcing its services in this area to Puerto Rico, the US Virgin Islands, Haiti, Curacao and Aruba that had commenced in 1971.

Boeing 767s were ordered in 1978 and in 1982 AA's first transatlantic service was flown to Frankfurt and Paris, followed in

Normally based at AA's San Juan hub, this Boeing 727 is seen at turnaround on its daily service to St Lucia's international airport at Hewanorra, on the southern tip of this Caribbean island.

One of the older DC-10-10s in AA's fleet, N126AA, on finals to land at their Miami hub.

May by its first Dallas/Fort Worth to London (Gatwick) using B767-200ERs.

Following deregulation in 1978 AA started a major route-expansion policy in 1979. Its last Boeing 707 was retired in 1981. AA also started to develop its hubs, its first at Dallas/Fort Worth being formally established in June 1981 and others at Chicago, Miami, Nashville, Raleigh/Durham and San Juan following during the 1980s. AA flew its 500-millionth passenger in May 1982.

On 19 May 1982 the airline's stockholders voted to approve a plan to reorganise the company so that a holding company, AMR Corporation, became the parent company of American Airlines, Inc. In 1984 came the inauguration of the first American Eagle commuter airline network, aimed at providing feeds from smaller towns and cities to the newly established hubs and some of the other larger airports that AA served – these airlines became subsidiaries, AMR Eagle, Inc. Airbus A300-600ERs joined the fleet in 1987 and in July, to boost the airline's presence on the US west coast, it took over AirCal. In 1989 AA ordered more new aircraft, eight McDonnell-Douglas MD-11s and seventy-five Fokker F100s, both types with order options for forty-two and seventy-five respectively. Their first new Boeing 757-200 entered service in 1989.

The demise of Eastern Air Lines enabled AA to acquire the rights to fly to twenty cities in fifteen Central and South American countries in 1990, expanding Eastern's former Miami hub significantly to cope. By 27 March 1991 AA had flown its one-billionth passenger. In May AA concluded the purchase of TWA's London (Heathrow) slots, sold by TWA to avert a financial crisis within that airline (Chapter 11 bankruptcy protection).

By 1994 AA was providing scheduled services to 306 cities across the US, Mexico, the Caribbean, South and Central America, Asia and Europe. These included 131 non-stop flights per week in the US–UK market. AA signed one of its first major code-share agreements in May 1996 with Singapore Airlines. This was quickly followed in June by the announcement of the proposed British Airways (BA)/AA alliance that would have given the two airlines control of 60% of the flights between the UK and the US. Many other airlines raised objections and disquiet at this proposed alliance. USAir (now US Airways) terminated its code-share and marketing agreement with BA, and started legal proceedings against BA, alleging a breach of trust and unfair competition. In the meantime, in 1998 US Airways signed an important marketing agreement with AA, but this falls short of a major code-share or alliance.

In 1996 AA placed a huge 103-aircraft order with Boeing worth up to $6.6 billion and placed options on a further 527 aircraft for delivery over the next twenty years. These include the airline's first twelve Boeing 777-200s, Boeing 757s and Boeing 737NGs (next generation). The first 777s and 737-800s were introduced into service during 1999. On 11 March 1999 AA acquired Business Express Airlines, a forty-three aircraft (Saab 340) commuter operator whose services were concentrated on feeding and linking the big conurbations in the US northeast, integrating them into the American Eagle network. On 31 August 1999 AA assimilated the routes and aircraft of Reno Air in an attempt to consolidate its position against increasing competition in the western states of the US. AA's total active fleet numbered 700 jet aircraft at the end of 1999, making AA at the time the largest airline in the US in terms of fleet size. It was also largest in terms of revenue ($20,110 million) although only second to United in terms of RPKs.

With the backdrop of the bustle of Los Angeles International Airport (LAX), one of AA's DC-10-10s about to touch down. This aircraft, N123AA, is about to be sold to Federal Express (FedEx).

RIGHT:
AA now have 102 Boeing 757s in their fleet, all 757-223 models, called 'Luxury Jets'.

BELOW:
A pair of newly delivered AA 757-223s during a night-stop at Orange County/John Wayne Airport to the south of Los Angeles in 1990.

Pictured amidst a variety of other international traffic at London (Heathrow) in July 1992, is an AA Boeing 767-323ER. This long-range type first entered service with AA in February 1988.

AA's dominance in serving the islands of the Caribbean, both inter-island and from the US, is emphasised by this gathering at Barbados in 1997. A 757 in the foreground and two of a fleet of thirty-five Airbus A300B-600Rs behind; the Airbus fleet being the exception to the bare, polished metal livery.

ABOVE:
The polished metal colours of AA's aircraft, as exemplified by this Boeing 767-323ER, have been a feature of the airline's identity for nearly thirty years.

LEFT:
With the rugged desert backdrop at Palm Springs, California, AA's MD-82 N400AA lifts off on a flight to San Jose.

In a hybrid colour scheme following AA's August 1999 take-over of Reno Air, this ex-Reno Air MD-83 is seen on the ramp at the famous Nevada gambling town that gave the airline its name, with the Nuggett and Hilton hotels beyond.

Landing at Reno, this AA MD-83 still wears the attractive Reno Air livery, but with just small AA titles on the tail to give away its new ownership in September 1999.

N753RA, an ex-Reno Air MD-87, one of twenty-five MD-82, -83, -87 and -90 aircraft that AA acquired in 1999 as part of its $124 million purchase price for this former Nevada-based airline.

ABOVE:
Frantic activity around AA's MD-83 N599AA during turnaround at San Diego – catering goes in and out of a special door on the aircraft's right-hand side whilst passengers board on the left.

RIGHT:
From July 1991 AA took delivery of its Fokker F100s for short/medium routes up to 1000 miles in length. N1403M is seen here taxying in Delta 'territory' at Atlanta Hartsfield International.

OPPOSITE:
A stone's throw from where it was manufactured at the McDonnell-Douglas plant at Long Beach, California, AA's MD-82 (N516AM) noses in at Long Beach after a flight from San Francisco.

With ramp temperatures at over 100 degrees F, a huge compressor/blower is attached to this AA Fokker F100 at Charlotte, North Carolina in an attempt to keep the aircraft cool for boarding passengers.

Passengers boarding an American Eagle ATR-72-212 at Chicago-O'Hare in 1992. One of these ATR-72s had a fatal crash, allegedly caused by severe icing whilst holding to land at Chicago, which caused AA and American Eagle to redeploy these aircraft to warmer parts of their network during the higher-risk winter months.

LEFT:
In the idyllic sub-tropical setting of the Caribbean island of St Lucia, an American Eagle ATR-72 back-tracks on the single runway, past the harbour entrance at Castries (Vigie), prior to its take-off.

American Eagle redeployed some of its ATR-42s and 72s to its Caribbean feeder network in the cold northern winter. Here an ATR-72 shares ramp space with a LIAT DHC-6 at St Lucia's Castries (Vigie) airport.

ABOVE:
American Eagle has a fleet of thirty-eight ATR-72s, twenty-six of the smaller 72-200s and twelve of the larger 72-500s. N431AT is an ATR-72-212, seen being serviced on the AA ramp at Tampa, Florida. These are all scheduled to be replaced by CRJ-700 jets from 2001 onwards.

LEFT:
American Eagle operates the world's largest fleet of Saab 340s (115 aircraft). AA announced in late 1999 that it would start to phase these out of its fleet, to be replaced by Embraer ERJ-135s and 145s.

25

ABOVE:
AA Boeing 757s at Miami, the airline's crossroads from mainland US to both the Caribbean and Latin America. Miami was ranked seventh in the US in 1998 in terms of aircraft movements, a significant proportion of them being AA and American Eagle, with 189 daily jet and 79 Eagle departures. In 1998 AA boarded 20,150,000 passengers at Miami.

BELOW:
A trio of AA Boeing 767s nosed-in at London Gatwick's South Terminal in April 1997.

LEFT:
A pair of MD-82s seen nearest and a Boeing 727, the mainstay of the AA domestic jet fleet that serves the Florida city of Tampa.

BELOW:
AA introduced Boeing 777s on its services to Gatwick in summer 1999.

United Airlines

Pacific Air Transport was founded in 1926 by Vern Gorst as an ancillary to his bus company, to bid for one of the US west coast CAM airmail routes between Los Angeles and Seattle. Varney Air Lines was another, along with Boeing Air Transport. All carried occasional passengers, but it was airmail that was their bread and butter. In October 1928 Pacific Air Transport was merged with Boeing Air Transport and the Pratt & Whitney Aircraft Company to become United Aircraft & Transport Company (UATC). UATC then bought out Stout Air Services. Challenging UATC were several other rivals, including Varney Air Lines and Maddux Air Lines, both part of the Keys Group. By 1929 UATC linked four main companies, the Boeing Airplane Company, Boeing Air Transport, Pacific Air Transport and Pratt & Whitney, soon to be joined by National Air Transport and Varney Air Lines. On 1 July 1931 United Airlines, Inc. was created as a management company for Boeing Air Transport, Pacific Air Transport, National Air Lines

United started as an airmail company, Pacific Air Transport, in 1926. By 1929 the company was flying Travelair 4000s between Los Angeles and Seattle. Retired United captain Lonnie Autry restored this Travelair in 1990–97 in PAT's original CAM 8 colours.

and Varney Air Lines. After several route and aircraft developments a separate business entity, United Airlines, was formed on 1 May 1934 from these four constituent companies. United had already forged ahead of the rivals by ordering and operating the then revolutionary Boeing 247 ten-passenger airliner.

June 1934's passing by congress of the Air Mail Act had a devastating effect on United as it effectively forbade the affiliation of airlines and aircraft manufacturers. This dented the airline's growth and development and allowed rivals such as TWA and American the opportunity to inaugurate schedules on some of the prime routes that United had formerly flown. United introduced its first DC-3 in 1936, used on the inaugural flight of its New York to Chicago service. United then collaborated with other major US airlines and Douglas in the development of the four-engined DC-4, although with the onset of war the airline did not take delivery of the DC-4, instead the USAAF taking on the aircraft as the Douglas C-54 Skymaster. During the war over half of United's sixty-nine aircraft fleet were redeployed into the US Army.

Post-war, United acquired DC-6s and flew them coast-to-coast from 1947 onwards, as well as linking San Francisco with Honolulu. In 1948 United inaugurated the airline industry's first

United was one of the launch customers for the Boeing 777 and flew the first revenue service of the type between Washington/Dulles International and London (Heathrow) in June 1995.

true hub operation at Denver. Other types that United ordered and flew in the late 1940s and early 1950s were the Boeing Stratocruiser, Convair 340 and Douglas DC-7. Its landmark order was in 1955 though, when it was launch customer for the new Douglas DC-8 jet, although they did not enter service until 1959; eleven Boeing 720s were also ordered in 1957 for service entry in 1960. Most revolutionary though, in that it was a European-built aircraft, United put the first of twenty Sud Aviation SE 210 Caravelle jets into service in 1961. In the same year the merger of Capital Airlines and United was approved, making United the largest airline in the world, with the exception of Aeroflot, and having a fleet of 267 aircraft that served 116 cities within the US and Canada.

In 1969 a new holding company, UAL Inc., was formed and United Airlines became a wholly owned subsidiary. The restructuring under the UAL Corporation was finally completed in 1988, United Airlines being the principal subsidiary. The first international services (other than to Canada) commenced in 1980 and in 1983 United flew its first true international service, a nonstop between the US and Tokyo. The first Boeing 767-200s were delivered in 1983. Further international expansion was possible in 1986 after the $715 million purchase of PanAm's Pacific Division. It was also the time when commuter airlines Air Wisconsin, Aspen and WestAir became franchised airlines as United Express.

Huge aircraft orders also followed as United commenced services to Europe in 1989, quickly consolidating its position in the US–UK market with the purchase in 1991 of PanAm's London (Heathrow) slots and expansion of service to South America the following year. United's order for Boeing 777s made it one of the launch customers for the type and the first revenue service for a 777 was a United Washington–Heathrow flight in June 1995. United has quickly become the largest US airline at Heathrow.

An important employee stock ownership plan (ESOP) was approved by United's shareholders in July 1994, making United the largest majority employee-owned company in the world. As part of this plan, as long as employees own 20% plus (currently it is estimated they own around 50% plus) of UAL stock, employees will continue to hold 55% of the voting rights. It was this 1994 ESOP that enabled United to develop its west coast 'airline-within-an-airline', the low-fare subsidiary Shuttle by United. Shuttle's first services were in October 1994. By 1998 Shuttle accounted for 466 daily departures flying over 40,000 passengers a day, was boarding over fourteen million passengers and flying a dedicated Boeing 737-300 and 737-500 fleet numbering sixty aircraft.

United has also dominated the alliance 'industry' announcing the creation of its Star Alliance in May 1997 in conjunction with Lufthansa, SAS, Air Canada and Thai Airways. In the airline's own right it now carries nearly nine million passengers on 70,000 international flights each year – this is part of its overall 87.2 million passenger total. In terms of RPK United Airlines is the largest of the 'Big Six'. Its proposed buy-out of US Airways, announced in May 2000, would make it the world's largest airline.

A Pratt & Whitney PW4000-engined United 777-222 at Heathrow in 1997. The 777 is the world's largest and heaviest twin-jet and received FAA certification in April 1995. One month later United took delivery of its first aircraft, N777UA.

Not quite Hong Kong but still an interesting approach, San Diego's Lindbergh Field in southern California; a United Boeing 727 is on short-finals to land.

LEFT:
N7458U Boeing 727-222 continues to fly with United in 1999 despite the airline's programme to phase out these older tri-jets. The fleet still numbers seventy-five of the type.

BELOW:
United took delivery of its first Boeing 727 N7620U in May 1968. The airline has operated a total of two hundred and thirty-one 727s of all types since then, this one taxying at Atlanta.

United Boeing 737 tails at Minneapolis/St Paul, the airline's total 737 fleet of all types numbering 182 aircraft. They are accompanied on this concourse by American Airlines Fokker F100s.

Photographed at the palm tree fringed Fort Lauderdale/Hollywood International airport in Florida, is one of United's Boeing 757-222s.

United was one of the first successful operators of a low-cost, airline-within-an-airline concept with its west coast Shuttle by United. Various liveries and letter styles have been adopted for the 737 Shuttle aircraft, this one a Boeing 737-322.

A different Shuttle by United lettering style on a new Boeing 737-522 at San Diego. The size of the Shuttle operation is staggering, with fourteen million passengers being carried in 1998.

Another different Shuttle livery adopted for N394UA, a Boeing 737-322. The Shuttle – as a separate entity – ranks third in terms of RPKs (revenue passenger kilometres) in US regional airlines, behind Alaska Airlines and American Trans Air.

ABOVE:
Sporting the Star Alliance logo behind the cockpit window, Airbus A320-232 N407UA at the gate at Tampa, Florida. United has a fleet of fifty-three A320s, with a further thirty-three on order, as well as A319s.

RIGHT:
Ideal for the stringent noise restrictions at John Wayne/Orange County airport in California, United's Airbus A320-232 N407UA.

United started taking delivery of its first Airbus A319-131s in 1997. It now has twenty-eight in service with a further nineteen on order; this example, N823UA, pictured with the characteristic hillside back-drop at San Diego's Lindbergh Field.

United heads up one of the strongest and most diverse alliance groups, the Star Alliance. Initially six airlines were involved and in 1998 one of these, SAS of Scandinavia painted one of its Boeing 767-383ERs in a special Star Alliance scheme, the United Airlines portion in the centre section above the wings.

RIGHT:
Despite Delta's dominance at Atlanta, other airlines of the 'Big Six' complement Delta's services, including United, whose Boeing 737-322 N349UA is framed by one of their Boeing 727s.

ABOVE:
Skywest of Utah began operations in 1972. In 1986 it became a Delta Airlines Connection carrier to feed Delta's Salt Lake City hub. On 1 October 1997 Skywest signed a marketing agreement with United Airlines to become a United Express carrier providing services to United's Los Angeles, San Francisco, Seattle/Tacoma and Portland hubs. Its fleet includes ninety-two Embraer EMB-120ER Brasilias.

BELOW:
Demonstrating the relationship between Mainline United and their United Express carriers – of which there are currently six – at John Wayne/Orange County airport in California, a mainline A320 passes a Skywest EMB-120 Brasilia being prepared for departure.

Delta Air Lines

Delta's beginnings were unique compared to the other airlines of the 'Big Six'; the world's first crop dusting operation, Huff-Daland Dusters, at Macon, Georgia formed in 1924. The company moved the following year to Monroe, Louisiana but, when the spraying season was over, diversified by establishing an operation in Peru. Here C.E. Woolman, who now owned the twenty-five aircraft aerial crop dusting company, first won the rights to fly airmail on a 1500-mile route between Peru and Ecuador. In Monroe a group of businessmen, along with Woolman, established an aviation company in 1928, naming it Delta Air Services after the geographical area in which it mainly operated, the Mississippi delta. Delta's first passenger service between Love Field, Dallas and Jacksonville, Mississippi was flown in June 1929. Competition, even in those days, was considerable, the newly formed American Airways being the main rival. Delta retrenched in the early 1930s, getting back into crop dusting, until in 1934 as the Delta Air Corporation, it successfully bid for one of the new revised airmail routes between Dallas and Charleston, South Carolina.

Named Delta Air Lines, the airline flew its first service on 4 July 1934. By 1935 Woolman ordered five Lockheed Model 10s and

Mainstay of Delta's international services and many of the higher-density domestic routes for many years, the Lockheed L1011 Tristar, the 'ten-eleven', was first delivered to Delta in December 1973. The type is used to link Atlanta with Ft Lauderdale, Florida where N754DL, a L1011-500 is pictured.

although smaller than rival airlines' aircraft, they suited the traffic levels and routes. Only in 1940 did Delta start flying surplus American Airlines DC-2s, followed at the end of the year by its first DC-3s, one of which, Ship 41 (NC28341) has been restored to flying condition by Delta at Atlanta. It first flew again after a five-year restoration programme in October 1999.

Atlanta became the new headquarters in 1941, more central to the airline's growing route network. The important routes from Atlanta to Miami via Jacksonville and from Cincinnati to Chicago were awarded to Delta after the war and on 18 December 1945 the airline officially became Delta Air Lines, this previously having been just an operating name for the Delta Air Corporation.

In March 1946 Delta flew its first DC-4 service, followed by an order for DC-6s to help beat off competition from Eastern Air Lines' Lockheed Constellations. In May 1953 the routes of the Chicago & Southern were transferred to Delta, adding the airline's first international services to Havana, Caracas and San Juan (Puerto Rico). Convair 340s were chosen as Delta's DC-3 replacement, followed by Convair 440s. A brief period of flying four ex-PanAm Constellations was followed in 1954 by the airline's first DC-7, primarily used on the important Chicago to Miami route. In September 1959 Delta introduced the DC-8 jet on its New York to Atlanta route and also at the time ordered Convair 880 jets. In December 1965, still loyal to Douglas, Delta put the first of its DC-9-14s into service, followed by larger DC-9-32s in 1967. The airline's first wide-body, the Lockheed L1011 Tristar entered service in 1968, complemented by the DC-10 between

1972 and 1975. The Boeing 747 did not suit Delta's route structure and so only five were ordered, operating between 1970 and 1977. Delta took over Northeast Airlines in August 1972, and thereby acquired its first Boeing 727s.

When the longer range L1011-500 became available Delta was the first of the non-traditional US carriers to win rights to fly trans-atlantic. It flew its first scheduled Atlanta to London (Gatwick) service in April 1978 – Delta had been flying charter services to the UK from the 1960s with DC-8-33s bought from PanAm.

Severe post-deregulation competition affected Delta in the early 1980s, although as launch customer for the new Boeing 767-232 it faced a huge dilemma. The airline's employees came to the rescue, and rather than face redundancy, responded by raising $30 million to fund the purchase of their first 767. It entered service in March 1983 and in tribute to the airline's employees was named *Spirit of Delta* (see the front cover picture), a name it still proudly carries. Competition from Eastern Air Lines at Delta's Atlanta base was still considerable, but Delta's management knew they had to invest in new aircraft and placed orders for their first Boeing 757 and McDonnell-Douglas MD-82s. In 1988 MD-11s were ordered, primarily as Tristar replacements and to enhance the airline's services from the US to Europe and Asia.

Delta's first code-share agreement with a commuter airline was signed in May 1984 with Atlantic Southeast Airlines. They provided feed to Delta at Atlanta from twenty-one smaller cities in Georgia, Alabama, Mississippi, Tennessee, and North and South Carolina.

As part of the consolidation of the US airline industry Delta took over Western Air Lines in 1987, gaining a major foothold in the western US as a result and acquiring more Boeing 727s and its first Boeing 737s. Delta benefited considerably from the demise of Eastern, not only through acquisition of airport gates, routes and passengers but also of ex-Eastern Tristars. When PanAm went bankrupt in 1991, Delta acquired its transatlantic routes, its fleet of Airbus A310s, and the airline's Frankfurt hub. Delta also acquired the former PanAm Shuttle operation in September 1991, the high frequency guaranteed-seat operation linking New York, Boston and Washington. Partly as a result of this, Delta's international capacity grew by 33% during 1993.

'Fly Delta Jets' is a remnant from the 1960s and the early days of Delta's operation of DC-8s on the Atlanta to New York route in competition with Eastern Air Lines. The sign survives at Atlanta Hartsfield International airport, as another Delta jet, an ex-Western Airlines Boeing 727-247 N831WA, touches down. A further revised livery, which involves the omission of the words 'Air Lines' from the fuselage titling and a new tail design, was unveiled in March 2000.

By 1995 the Delta aircraft fleet numbered 550 aircraft. It was the first year that the airline had recorded a profit for some time, largely as a result of Chairman Ronald Allen's 'Leadership 7.5' programme. Orders for new aircraft, previously put on hold, were reinstated, Boeing 767-300ERs, Boeing 737-300s and MD-90s. With the 1996 Olympic Games in Atlanta, the airline was the official airline of the games. It also announced that it was to start phasing out its L1011 fleet and ordered additional 767-300ERs.

The last years of the 1990s have seen profits at Delta soar, almost in parallel with the numbers of passengers it has carried and the growth of its Atlanta Hartsfield hub. In 1996 Delta's low-cost unit, Delta Express started its Boeing 737-200 services centred on Orlando. A new identity and colour scheme was first adopted by Delta in 1997, the year that Leo F. Mullin took over as President and CEO and also the first year that Delta carried over 100 million passengers. A major development of new services into the Caribbean, Central and South America has been in progress during 1998 and 1999 as Delta signed a twenty-year exclusivity deal with Boeing for the supply of up to 644 new aircraft. These included the Boeing 777, the first of which entered service during the summer of 1999, despite problems over pilot contracts for their operation and the deferment of some deliveries of the type. Delta also acquired both Atlantic Southeast Airlines and Cincinnati-based Comair in 1999, formerly independent Delta Connection commuter operators. The proposed merger with Continental Airlines failed in 1997 but Delta concluded its important alliance with Air France in 1999. Delta is now the world's largest airline in terms of passengers carried, a staggering 105.5 million in 1999.

During the 1970s Delta took delivery of L1011 Tristars, Boeing 747s and DC-10s, making it the only operator of all three available wide-body jets of the time. Delta plans to phase out all L1011s by the end of 2000, replacing them mostly with Boeing 767s.

Delta acquired its Delta Shuttle operation and fleet of Boeing 727s in September 1991 as part of a $416 million deal with the ailing PanAm that also included what remained of PanAm's transatlantic routes. The Delta Shuttle boarded over two million passengers in 1997 and operates sixty-four daily scheduled flights between New York and Washington or New York and Boston. Delta has announced that its Shuttle 727s will be replaced by sixteen Boeing 737-800s from July 2000.

ABOVE:
Paulette Corbin and 'Skip' Barnette headed the small Delta employee team who worked on establishing Delta Express in 1996. The airline unit now serves over 15 cities with over 150 daily flights, none of which touch Delta's hub airports such as Atlanta. This Boeing 737-232 N315DL has just been rolled out in the new Delta and Delta Express livery in March 1999.

RIGHT:
Operating in the mountains of the Sierra Nevada at Reno, Nevada this Boeing 737-3B7 N947WP was acquired by Delta following the collapse of Colorado Springs-based Western Pacific Airlines.

LEFT:
Delta Air Lines introduced its new colour scheme as depicted on this Boeing 737-3B7 in 1997, designed by London-based Landor Associates and the first change in livery for thirty-five years. 1997 was also the year that Delta first carried over 100 million passengers in one year, the historic passenger being Margaret Mack, who boarded Delta flight no. 680 to Atlanta at Dallas/Fort Worth on 22 December. A further new revision of Delta's livery was unveiled in March 2000.

BELOW:
Another Boeing 737 movement at Atlanta Hartsfield International, now named Atlanta Worldport. This is 737-35B N224DA, one of thirteen 737-300s in Delta's fleet.

RIGHT:
Climbing away at Atlanta Worldport, N128DL, a Boeing 767-332. Delta has seventy-nine of the type in service plus a further seventeen on order and eleven on option. These are 300 series models, the basic 332 and the 332ER (extended range).

OPPOSITE:
New red, blue and white house colours of Delta on the tails of two Boeing 767-300s on the international concourse at Atlanta Worldport.

BELOW:
Some of Delta's thirteen Boeing 737-35Bs are ex-Germania Flug (a German charter airline based at Cologne) aircraft, acquired to make up a short-term shortfall in the fleet. N224DA is ex-D-AGED.

Delta's first Boeing 767-332 was delivered in November 1986. Initially configured with 252 passenger seats, 24 in first and 228 in coach, these have now changed with the airline's 1999 introduction of its new Business Elite *class and feature fewer* coach *seats, and more* Business Elite.

ABOVE:
With the wing-tip winglets raised, giving maximum lift, MD-11, N801DE, the first delivered to Delta, lifts off from Atlanta Worldport. Prior to the delivery of its own aircraft, Delta leased two MD-11s which first entered service in November 1990.

OPPOSITE:
Delta has one of the largest and most modern dedicated paint shops at its Atlanta TOC – this McDonnell-Douglas MD-11 is receiving a 'make-over' to the new livery in March 1999.

LEFT:
The Captain and First Officer of this MD-11 feed navigational route data into the aircraft's navigation system and prepare the aircraft for push-back from the stand.

Taxying past the South Terminal at London (Gatwick), is MD-11 N809DE. The type has also been modified internally from three-class to two-class seating, like the 767-332ERs. The MD-11 now features fifty seats in Business Elite and 197 in Coach.

Named Centennial Spirit in 1996 when Delta was official airline of the 1996 Olympic Games in Atlanta, this MD-11 was also painted in a special Centennial Olympic livery. It subsequently reverted to the regular Delta livery, but retained its name.

With Douglas jets from an earlier era behind, a Delta MD-88, N919DL, taxies in after landing at Miami.

RIGHT:
Atlantic Southeast Airlines (ASA) became a franchised Delta Connection airline in May 1984 when it started a code-share agreement with Delta. In 1999 Delta acquired ASA as an essential element of its regional operations and a feed to its Atlanta hub. ASA's first Bombardier/ Canadair Regional jets were delivered in late 1997.

BELOW:
Delta's initial 20% shareholding in ASA increased to 28% and in May 1999 the $700 million deal was finally concluded for Delta to purchase ASA as a wholly owned subsidiary.

The Airbus A320 is now being complemented in the Northwest fleet by the delivery of the first of its order for fifty of the smaller A319s.

OPPOSITE:
Because of the versatility and range of the Airbus A320, Northwest uses the type for its transcontinental flights in the US, linking to its hubs, particularly Minneapolis/St Paul (the Twin Cities). This A320 is preparing for departure from Reno, Nevada, destination: the Twin Cities.

RIGHT:
With two flight-deck crew, capacity for 150 passengers and a range of up to 2930 nautical miles, the Airbus A320 has US coast-to-coast range. This Northwest A320-212 is landing at Los Angeles International.

BELOW:
Northwest's domestic A320 competition at Los Angeles International (LAX) includes low-fare Southwest and American Airlines, photographed with an ex-Reno Air MD-90. Northwest are now using American Eagle flights in a code-share agreement to provide feed from seven Californian cities into LAX.

ABOVE:
Mesaba Airlines is a Minneapolis/St Paul-based Northwest Airlink airline, and first signed a co-operative agreement with Northwest in December 1984 to become a Northwest Airlink carrier. Following a 1997 ten-year code-share agreement between Mesaba and Northwest, Mesaba has started re-equipping with BAe RJ 85s, acquired by Northwest and leased to Mesaba. Here two RJ 85s occupy the gates at Minneapolis/St Paul in June 1998.

LEFT:
Northwest was the first big US airline to order the Airbus A320. It has remained loyal to the European manufacturer and in addition to the A320s and A319s on order, has ordered sixteen of the larger, long-range A330-300s. A delivery date for these A330s has yet to be finalised.

Mainstay of the Northwest Airlink fleet of Mesaba for several years, its DHC-8s have all now been disposed of. This DHC-8 is executing a classic crosswind landing at Detroit in 1997, wing-down into the wind.

ABOVE:
Twenty-one Douglas DC-10-40s fly in the Northwest fleet, complemented by a further twenty DC-10-30s. The -40s are fitted with P & W JT-9D-20 engines, in contrast to the -30s' GE CF6-50Cs.

BELOW:
Over the 'piano keys' at the end of Detroit's' runway 21R (right) is a Northwest DC-10-30. Northwest has added further second-hand DC-10s to its fleet in recent years, including ex-Swissair, Korean and Thai aircraft. Compare the shape of the tail-mounted engine nacelle of this DC-10-30 with that of the DC-10-40 above.

LEFT:
Forty-eight Boeing 757-251s are currently flown by Northwest, with a further ten on order. The first of the type was delivered to the airline in February 1985 when it was named 'Northwest Orient'. This aircraft, N519US, was part of their initial order for twenty of the type.

OPPOSITE:
Being guided by traditional methods for the last few metres of its arrival at the gate, a DC-10-40 slowly noses its way forward.

BELOW:
Atmospheric shot of an early-morning Northwest Boeing 757-251 arriving at Minneapolis/St Paul – note the wing-tip vortices from the moist advection fog lying in the nearby Mississippi river valley.

Northwest has been flying the Boeing 747 since June 1970, when its first 747-100 flew a schedule between Minneapolis/St Paul and New York. Since then the airline has operated the 747-200, the 747-200F (freighter) and the 747-400. Here N628US lines up for take-off at Los Angeles International for a flight to Honolulu.

Northwest took delivery of its first three dedicated 747-200Fs in 1975 amidst scepticism from other mainline US airlines. Northwest's established links across the Pacific and the burgeoning industrial growth in SE Asia helped to fuel the operation's success. Their current nine-aircraft 747-200F cargo fleet contributes over 8% of the airline's total revenue.

LEFT:
So dominant are Northwest and its aircraft at its Detroit hub that it is sometimes called 'The Red Sea'. There are over 360 daily jet departures and 148 Northwest Airlink departures from here during an average day, accounting for over 1000 daily movements (departures and arrivals).

Northwest's alliance with Dutch airline KLM has benefited significantly from the 1993 granting of anti-trust immunity. The two airlines claim that their alliance has helped boost their annual growth from 5% to nearly 15%.

ABOVE:
A variety of Northwest aircraft types nosed-in at the Gold Concourse at Minneapolis/St Paul in June 1995.

BELOW:
Such is the size of Northwest's operation at Detroit and the extent of its growth (it now handles over 32 million passengers a year) that the Detroit Airport Authority has commenced a $1.6 billion expansion programme for new terminals and other facilities.

RIGHT:
It is the season of mists and mellow fruitfulness as a Northwest Airbus A320 arrives amidst dramatically lit ground mist at Minneapolis/St Paul.

BELOW:
Northwest DC-10-30, N237NW, was painted in a dual NW/KLM scheme in 1999 to emphasise the strength of the alliance between the two airlines.

US Airways

The name US Airways was not adopted until 1997. It was the culmination of a diverse amalgamation of smaller airlines and air operators over the last sixty-three years, the oldest of which was founded in 1937 as All American Aviation. They won contracts in 1938 to deliver mail by air, flying as All American Airways, to fifty-four communities in Pennsylvania, Delaware, Maryland, West Virginia and Ohio. They used Stinson SR-10 Reliant aircraft and by 1940 had increased the number of routes they served and the number of communities to eighty-seven.

In 1948 the Civil Aeronautics Board awarded All American its first temporary three-year licence to operate passenger schedules, initially using Beech 18s and then DC-3s. The first scheduled service between Washington DC and Pittsburgh was flown in March 1949. This was the same year as Pacific Southwest Airlines (PSA) flew their first DC-3 service in California between San Diego and Oakland. In 1948 Piedmont Airlines flew its first scheduled DC-3 service between Wilmington and Cincinnati – this was a development from Piedmont Aviation, Inc., an aircraft sales and service company, that had been formed at Winston-Salem, North Carolina in July 1940.

All American Airways changed its name to Allegheny Airlines in 1953. The airline soon started to retire DC-3s, replacing them with Martin 2-0-2s, followed by Convair 340s and 440s in the early 1960s as its area of service concentrated on flying from smaller communities to the big north-eastern US cities of Boston, Philadelphia, Pittsburgh and Washington DC. Through the 1950s Piedmont's services centred on Winston-Salem and Charlotte,

North Carolina, turbo-prop Fairchild F27s and Martin 4-0-4s replacing this airline's DC-3s.

A series of mergers helped the growth of both Allegheny and Piedmont. The Turner Aeronautical Corporation became Turner Airlines and then Lake Central Airlines – Lake Central was taken over by Allegheny in 1968. The Airline Division of Robinson Aviation became Mohawk Airlines and they agreed to merge with Allegheny in 1972. Piedmont, meanwhile, developed from a local to a regional airline and established Charlotte as its main operating hub in 1981. Piedmont had ordered Boeing 737s and in 1984 its first Fokker F28 entered service. The airline's F28 fleet grew significantly in 1985 when it took over Empire Airlines. In June 1987 Piedmont launched its first transatlantic service from Charlotte to London (Gatwick). By 1988 Piedmont was the US's largest Boeing 737 operator, was launch customer for the Boeing 737-400 and had subsidiary hubs at Baltimore/Washington, Dayton and Syracuse, as well as an intensive intra-state scheduled F28 network in Florida.

In October 1979 Allegheny Airlines changed its name to USAir.

The twelve Boeing 767-200ERs in US Airways' fleet are all ex-Piedmont Airlines aircraft. Piedmont used them to launch its first transatlantic services in June 1987. British Airways took over this route from USAir under an alliance that was nullified in 1996. US Airways started flying the Charlotte (North Carolina) to London (Gatwick) route again in June 1999 in competition with BA, which uses Boeing 777s.

Gatwick's characteristic jet-blast wall provides a backdrop to the arrival of a US Airways Boeing 767-200ER at the satellite of the South Terminal on one of its two daily services from Philadelphia.

Examples of the post-deregulation mergers, largely forced by the severe inter-airline competition and the need to consolidate operations, fleets and operational areas, soon followed for USAir. First in 1988 it was PSA, an airline which had concentrated on development of services in the west of the US, had grown to a fifty-five-plus, all jet aircraft fleet and which was boarding over one million passengers a month. Piedmont soon followed as USAir completed the merger by August 1989. USAir's network now embraced the whole of the US as well as transatlantic services to Europe.

The diverse and largely inherited aircraft fleet, along with the traditional and difficult operational area of the US northeast did nothing to help USAir's profitability. In January 1996 Stephen Wolf was appointed as Chairman and CEO of the USAir Group and set about a major revamping of the airline. Its fleet rationalisation was high on the priority list and the huge 400-aircraft order placed for Airbus A320 family aircraft by Wolf in 1996 was a sign of things to come. Profitability returned and the 1997 image makeover started with the airline being renamed US Airways. Amongst many radical and far-reaching changes since then, the development of the Philadelphia hub and the growth of

international services to Europe from this hub have probably been most significant. Development of further international services to Europe from Charlotte is also in progress. Following BA's 1999 withdrawal of its Pittsburgh–London service US Airways now operates on this route. US Airways has also developed the US's largest associated commuter network – ten smaller airlines operating under the US Airways Express banner, the most recent recruit being Colgan Air.

In 2000 US Airways took delivery of its first Airbus A330-300 and these will start to replace the ex-Piedmont Boeing 767-200ERs used on transatlantic services. These Airbus aircraft are being complemented by continuous deliveries of new Airbus A321, A320 and A319 aircraft – A318 orders are also a possibility. Some of these will replace ageing Boeing 727s used on the US Airways Shuttle operation, a remnant of the former Trump Shuttle. These intensive, high frequency services operate between Boston, New York and Washington. Another rapidly growing element of the US Airways operation is their low-fare unit, MetroJet. Since June 1998 this has grown to a fifty-four-aircraft Boeing 737-200 fleet, linking up to thirty cities with over three hundred daily departures, all concentrated in the eastern half of the US and particularly, although not exclusively, feeding from the north-east into Florida. Biggest surprise though was the May 2000 announcement that United Airlines and US Airways would combine in a transaction valued at $11.6 billion.

76

The striking new colours of US Airways were introduced along with the airline's new name in February 1997 as part of airline Chairman Stephen Wolf's master-plan to revamp the airline. The dark upper and tail surfaces are called 'US blue' not black.

A fleet of thirty-four Boeing 757-200s flown by US Airways includes eleven ex-Eastern Air Lines 757s.

LEFT:
Landing at San Diego after a coast-to-coast flight from US Airways' Charlotte hub, a Boeing 757-200. The type first entered service with USAir in 1992, when they acquired ex-Eastern Air Lines Rolls-Royce RB 211-535S powered aircraft.

BELOW:
USAir's initial 1985 order for twenty Fokker F100s was the first for a North American customer and along with Swissair's order helped launch production of the type. Piedmont Airlines (and Empire which it acquired in 1986) was a Fokker F28 Fellowship operator, although all of the F28s that US Airways inherited have now been retired. The airline's F100 fleet now numbers forty aircraft. Six are seen here at the airline's Charlotte hub.

ABOVE:
Airbus A320 family aircraft are now starting to dominate US Airways' fleet following its order for up to 400 of the three types (A319, A320 and A321). They received the first of their order for thirty Airbus A330-300s in May 2000 as part of a programme to operate an all-Airbus fleet.

OPPOSITE:
After a heavy rainstorm the new 'US Dark-Blue' livery used for the upper fuselage surfaces by US Airways is shown to perfection on this Airbus A319 as it taxies slowly to the gate at Tampa, Florida.

RIGHT:
US Airways' first Airbus to enter service was A319 N700UW in November 1998. New A319 and A320 aircraft are now arriving at the rate of over two a month. A319-112 N705UW is pictured here at Tampa, in Florida, one of the first destinations to be served by the type.

Piedmont Airlines claimed to be the US's fastest-growing airline in the mid-1980s when it ordered twenty-five Boeing 737-400s, becoming the launch customer for the type. US Airways now has fifty-four of these CFM56-3B-powered, 146-seat jets in their fleet. N424US is pictured.

An Airbus A319 at push-back at Charlotte, North Carolina. Charlotte is the chosen location for a new US Airways training centre that will focus on the Airbus and house the airline's Airbus simulators.

An ex-USAir Boeing 737-301 rotates at take-off from US Airways' Charlotte hub.

Boeing 737s are currently the most numerous type in the US Airways fleet with 203 examples, 85 of them 737-300s as pictured. Eventually Airbus A320 family aircraft will overtake Boeings in the numerical stakes at US Airways.

ABOVE:
Taxying for departure at Ft Lauderdale in Florida, a US Airways Boeing 737-3B7.

BELOW:
The transition from one livery to another is a slow process with a fleet size numbering nearly 400 aircraft. This Boeing 737-3B7 is still in the old USAir colours. Aircraft first started to appear in US Airways' new livery in March 1997, but by the end of 1999 only 20% of the fleet still awaited their new paint job.

ABOVE:
US Airways' low-fare unit, MetroJet, flew its first service on 1 June 1998. MetroJet's aircraft are all Boeing 737-200s, transferred to MetroJet from the US Airways mainline fleet.

OPPOSITE:
With attrition from some stormy weather evident on the nose cone of this Boeing 737-301, still in USAir colours in July 1999, this aircraft will shortly enter US Airways' engineering facility at Tampa for its make-over. A Boeing 737-200 of low-fare unit MetroJet taxies in behind.

LEFT:
By early 2000 MetroJet expected to have a fleet of 54 Boeing 737-200s flying 300 daily flights and serving 26 cities, mainly in the eastern US. Their 737 aircraft have a one-class, 118-seat layout.

MetroJet's colours complement mainline US Airways', having crimson-red upper fuselage surfaces but retaining the 'US Dark-Blue' colours and US Airways' mainline logo on the tail. MetroJet was initially centred on Baltimore/Washington airport but has expanded since then, quite openly being a tool to tap new markets, but also to counter incursions into the eastern US by competitors such as Southwest and Delta Express. This MetroJet 737-200 is at Ft Lauderdale, Florida.

BELOW:

Although there are now ten US Airways Express commuter operators, three of these are wholly owned subsidiaries of US Airways and carry the historic names of the main antecedents of the airline, Piedmont, Allegheny and PSA. This is a Piedmont DHC-8-102, N998HA, at Tampa, shortly after its delivery to the airline in 1999.

ABOVE:
Another US Airways Express operator – albeit this aircraft is still in the former US Air Express colours – is Mesa Airlines, which has thirty-seven Raytheon/Beechcraft B1900Ds in its fleet.

BELOW:
The US Airways Express ramp at US Airways' Charlotte hub, with a Mesa Airlines CRJ Srs. 200ER regional jet sandwiched between DHC-8s of Piedmont (an ex-Henson aircraft). Mesa's CRJs were used to inaugurate a new Charlotte to Toronto (Canada) service in 1999. Other US Airways Express operators are now starting to operate regional jets, including Chautauqua Airlines with Embraer ERJ-145s.

ABOVE:
PSA Airlines Mk 2 was founded at Latrobe, Pennsylvania as Vee Neal Airlines. It became Jetstream International Airlines, then an affiliate of Piedmont Airlines in 1985 and then in 1988 a wholly owned subsidiary of USAir. The PSA name was adopted in November 1995, the airline now flying twenty-six Fairchild-Dornier 328-100s and with orders for fourteen more. This 328 is pictured at Washington's Ronald Reagan National airport.

RIGHT:
Florida is one of the largest markets in the US, headed by leisure travellers. US Airways' services, which span the US and particularly the eastern seaboard, are particularly strong in this market. Departures are seen here at Ft Lauderdale by both US Airways and MetroJet 737-200s, with an American Airlines MD-82 landing.

LEFT:
Philadelphia is the fourth-largest metropolitan area in the US with an estimated population of over five million served by only one airport – as part of the 1997 US Airways development plan, Philadelphia figured prominently for development. Here a mix of Boeing and MD aircraft are seen during an afternoon traffic 'bank' at Philadelphia in 1998.

BELOW:
Philadelphia was always an important hub for both Allegheny and USAir. It has been developed in recent years as one of US Airways' major hubs, particularly for international traffic to Europe, and now accounts for 398 daily mainline and Express departures. A Boeing 737-401, A319 and Boeing 757 are pictured at Philadelphia in November 1998.

Continental Airlines

In July 1934 Varney Air Services, operating as Varney Speed Lines, started operating its Lockheed Vegas on the route between Pueblo, Colorado and El Paso, Texas. Varney Airlines had been sold to United Air Lines in 1930. During 1937 three Lockheed 12s were added to the fleet, the year that the airline officially changed its name to Continental. During World War II Continental modified B-17s and B-29s at its new Denver facility, although its civilian operations had continued to expand modestly. By 1945 Continental's route network covered much of the southern mid-west US in a square bordered by Denver, Kansas City, San Antonio and El Paso. The airline was flying six DC-3s, had 400 employees and a 3000-mile route network serving twenty-six cities.

The first of five Convair 240s was ordered in 1946. In 1951 Continental entered into an interchange agreement with Braniff and American, another early example of airline alliances. Convair

340s and DC-6s were added to Continental's fleet and in 1953 Continental took over Pioneer Airlines, adding sixteen new cities to its expanding route network. By 1955 Continental had received authority to fly between Los Angeles and Chicago. The airline ordered DC-7s but also fifteen Vickers Armstrong V810 Viscounts, used to inaugurate turbo-prop services between Chicago, Kansas City and Los Angeles. Continental's first Boeing 707 service departed Los Angeles in June 1959, making the airline the third to introduce this new jet behind American and TWA.

The airline's emphasis changed with the 707s from essentially a short-haul network to a long-haul one, Boeing 720s being added in 1961 as the last of the airline's DC-3s were retired. In 1963 Continental moved its headquarters from Denver to Los Angeles and then won a lucrative contract to fly into SE Asia as part of the Vietnam War effort. DC-9s were ordered to replace the Viscounts, along with more 707s and the airline's first Boeing 727s. Continental started its first charter flights to Europe in the 1960s and in 1967 formed a Pacific Division, Air Micronesia (Air Mike for short), to fly inter-island schedules with Boeing 727s.

Boeing 747s were first delivered in 1970 following the adoption of the airline's new gold, red, orange and white colours. Douglas

In late 1999 Continental still had twenty-two Boeing 727s in their fleet, but, as with the other 'Big Six' airlines, the 727's days are numbered, in Continental's case following thirty-five years of service. This 727, seen landing at San Diego in 1996, has since been retired.

DC-10s were ordered soon after as services between Los Angeles and Honolulu commenced. Continental had been profitable every year but one since 1937, but with deregulation things changed dramatically, as they did with most other US airlines.

Houston in Texas began to figure more prominently in Continental's operations, particularly as the 'gateway' to the developing Mexican resorts on the Yucatan. In 1981 Frank Lorenzo's Texas Air Corporation began to acquire a controlling interest in Continental. However, losses spiralled upwards and a merger with Lorenzo's Texas International took place. It was not long before Lorenzo was forced to apply for Chapter 11 bankruptcy protection for Continental in September 1983. Cities served reduced from seventy-eight to twenty-five, employee numbers reduced from 12,000 to 4000 and negotiations with pilots and flight attendants failed. Non-unionised staff were employed and by the end of 1984 Continental had bounced back into profits, and also moved its headquarters from Los Angeles to its current location in Houston.

In 1985 Continental took delivery of its first Boeing 737s and 737-300s, as well as announcing an order for Airbus A300s, and inaugurated its daily Houston to London (Gatwick) service, as well as new services to Canada and Bali. The Texas Air Corporation (TAC) also bid $600 million for the ailing Eastern Air Lines. In June 1986 Continental emerged from Chapter 11 and TAC successfully bid for the New York (Newark)-based People Express, as well as most of the assets of Frontier Airlines. Continental Express was formed in 1987, an incorporation of ten smaller commuter-type airlines. New York Air was also taken over in 1987, consolidating Continental's dominant position at Newark and raising Continental to the US's third largest airline behind American and United.

With Frank Lorenzo's departure, but with the increased competition in the US and global markets and the effects of the Gulf War in 1990–91, Continental again filed for Chapter 11 bankruptcy protection. A revamped image, a heavy involvement

Like Continental, with its dwindling fleet of 727s, its Pacific subsidiary, Continental Micronesia also continues to fly thirteen of the type, including six 727 freighters for DHL. This 727 is seen taxying at Houston with a Continental Express commuter Raytheon/Beechcraft B1900D, N92539, biding its time.

with the Civil Reserve Air Fleet (CRAF) during the Gulf War and Continental was bouncing back, although under new CEO Robert Ferguson III the airline was drastically slimmed down, with fewer staff, fewer aircraft and fewer routes. Continental did not emerge from Chapter 11 protection until April 1993, but then started a fleet re-investment programme, ordering ninety-two new Boeings, 737s, 757s, 767s and 777s.

Continental has consolidated its position at Houston (now George Bush Intercontinental Airport) and at its other hubs at Newark and Cleveland, but is running down its Denver hub. As well as services to London (Gatwick), Continental also started a Newark to both Manchester and Birmingham (UK) service in 1995. The airline also signed an important alliance with Alitalia and in 1998 Northwest Airlines bought a 14% equity stake in Continental, and although Delta was also 'talking to' Continental, the Continental/Northwest tie-up has prospered, being a 'clean fit'. Northwest dominates the north-west from its Minneapolis and Detroit hubs, as well as by its strengths to the Orient and through KLM to Europe and beyond. Continental complements this coverage with its southern US and New York presence and offers serious competition to American in its Latin American services.

By 1998 Continental was the eleventh largest airline in the world in terms of revenue ($7,951 million), a huge 10.2% increase from the 1997 figure. Of the 'Big Six' its passenger growth figures in the first six months of 1999 were the highest with an 11.3% increase over the same 1998 period. During 1999 Continental carried 45.54 million passengers, an all-time record for the airline.

RIGHT:
A rocket-like departure from runway 09L (left) at Miami for Continental's MD-82, N14871 – it has sixty-nine MD-80s (81s, 82s and 83s) in its fleet as well as eleven older Douglas DC-9-32s.

BELOW:
The McDonnell-Douglas MD-80 series is an important element of Continental's domestic fleet. This MD-82 is at the gate at Houston George Bush Intercontinental Airport, the airline's main operating base since its 1984 move from Los Angeles.

A familiar sight at London's Gatwick airport for many years as a Continental Douglas DC-10-30 pushes back from the finger of the South Terminal in preparation for a morning departure to Newark. Continental flies daily services from Gatwick to Cleveland, Newark and Houston. It also flies daily from three other UK cities, Manchester, Birmingham and Glasgow, to Newark. Continental DC-10s overnight at Gatwick, when FLS Aerospace carry-out 'A'-check maintenance. Continental roster a different DC-10, from the 33 in their fleet, nearly every night.

Continental's thirty-three DC-10s have been the backbone of its long-haul fleet since the early 1970s, and although it flew Boeing 747s, these have all now been retired. N14063 at the gate at Houston, is configured in a 242-seat layout, with 38 seats in Business First and 204 in Coach. One of Continental's strengths from both Houston and Newark is its range of Latin American services with 500 departures a week.

Boeing is now the favoured airliner manufacturer of Continental. Some of these Boeing 757-224s, configured with the airline's Business First seating layout, have been used since 1 July 1999 on its new Cleveland to London (Gatwick) service, the airline's sixth daily service from the US to Gatwick.

Thirty-six Boeing 757-224s are now flying with Continental, part of a huge Boeing fleet rejuvenation plan following the airline's emergence from Chapter 11 protection in 1993. This aircraft, N12109, is landing at San Diego, California.

OPPOSITE:
Amongst the 179 Boeing 737 variants that Continental operates, there are 67 of the smallest type, the 737-524. This one is taxying after arrival at Houston. The 737-

500 series first flew in June 1989 and Boeing made its last delivery of the type ten years later, a total of 389 being delivered.

BELOW:
No mistaking the location with the US Capitol building beyond this Continental Boeing 737-524 as it lines up for take-off at an autumnal Washington Ronald Reagan National Airport.

RIGHT:
With an evening storm brewing off the Florida coast, Continental Boeing 737-524 prepares to line up at Ft Lauderdale for departure to Newark (New York).

OPPOSITE:
Like other airlines of the 'Big Six', Continental has consolidated much of its US domestic activity at its major hubs. These are at Cleveland (279 daily departures), Newark/New York (384 daily departures) and the biggest, Houston George Bush Intercontinental, with 522 daily departures. Continental's Boeing 737 fleet is dominant at all these hubs.

BELOW:
One of the first airlines to start Boeing 777 services to London (Gatwick) was Continental, which has been flying to the airport from Houston ever since 1985. The airline now flies twice daily between the two cities with its Boeing 777-224ERs.

ABOVE:
The huge and powerful General Electric GE90-90B engines fitted to Continental's Boeing 777-224ER fleet each give a 90,000-pound thrust. The aircraft cruises at 550mph and can carry 283 passengers (48 in Business First and 235 in Coach).

RIGHT:
Continental Express ordered 25 Raytheon/Beechcraft B1900Ds in 1994 following the retirement of its B1900Cs. Most were used for new services from Continental's Cleveland hub, but a few were deployed to Houston, where N81546 is pictured. It is expected that Embraer ERJ-135s will replace the B1900Ds.

It was Texas Air, Continental's then owner, which first ordered ATR-42s in 1987 for its various partner airlines, including Bar Harbor operating as Eastern Express. These aircraft were then transferred to Continental Express, becoming the mainstay of its operations at Houston along with Embraer EMB-120s.

The two Allison Rolls-Royce AE3007A turbofans fitted to Continental Express' Embraer ERJ-145s. The fuselage is basically a lengthened Brasilia structure and can carry fifty passengers. Continental Express also put the smaller, thirty-seven-seat ERJ-135 into service at its Cleveland hub on 23 July 1999.

Gulfstream International operates code-share services with Continental under the 'Continental Connection' name. Colgan Air did the same until its migration to become a US Airways Express operator in December 1999. Gulfstream operates a fleet of Raytheon/Beechcraft B1900Cs and DHC Dash 7s in Florida and the Bahamas, including 378 new weekly departures to four Caribbean destinations from San Juan, Puerto Rico. These three B1900Cs are pictured at Tampa, Florida.

Continental Express flew the first commercial Embraer ERJ-145 service on 6 April 1997. Continental Express first ordered up to 200 ERJ-145s in September 1996 and plans to move to an all-jet fleet. This ERJ-145 is pictured at Charlotte, North Carolina.

Displaying its current logo and identity is this Continental Boeing 757-234, N12109. The livery was first unveiled on 12 February 1991 on an Airbus A300 (since disposed of) at a ceremony at Houston and was intended to 'symbolise the airline's real and growing potential to link the countries of the globe together'.

RIGHT:
Continental McDonnell Douglas MD-82, N69826. With a fleet of sixty-nine MD-80 series aircraft representing nearly 20% of the fleet size, the type operates from Continental's hubs, largely replacing Boeing 727s, although carrying ten fewer passengers than the tri-jet. This MD-82 is about to depart Lindbergh Field, San Diego for Houston.

A mix of Continental Express aircraft types on their ramp at Houston George Bush Intercontinental Airport in Texas, where they account for 172 daily departures.

ABOVE:
1998 saw the last year of operations by Continental of its older Boeing 737-200 aircraft. These have all now been retired, N14245 seen rotating at take-off at Minneapolis/St Paul in June 1998.

OPPOSITE:
Continental's the name and the North American continent is the airline's 'backyard'. From 1937, when the Continental name replaced predecessor Varney Speed Lines, the airline has grown, despite the two hiccoughs of Chapter 11 in 1983 and 1991, to become the fifth-largest US airline in terms of revenue passenger kilometres, and seventh-largest in terms of number of passengers carried. Southwest Airlines was the sixth-largest in terms of passengers (57.5 million) in 1999.

RIGHT:
Continental Douglas DC-9-32 tails at Houston George Bush Intercontinental Airport in June 1996. Eleven of the type were still in service with Continental in October 1999, although their days of operational service must be numbered.

Appendix

The Big Six – Fast Facts

1) American Airlines
(Information correct to October 1999)

	Daily Departures			Airports Served
American Airlines	2,400	American Airlines		160
American Eagle	1,400	American Eagle		126
		Business Express		17
System Combined	3,800	System Combined (net of duplicates)		238

Daily Departures at Major Airports

City	Jet	Eagle	Total
Dallas/Fort Worth (Hub)	531	253	784
Chicago O'Hare (Hub)	336	157	493
Miami (Hub)	189	79	268
San Juan (Hub)	42	78	120

DESTINATIONS SERVED

Domestic
42 States in US, District of Columbia, Commonwealth of Puerto Rico, US Virgin Islands.

International
Anguilla, Antigua & Barbuda, Argentina, Aruba, Bahamas, Barbados, Belgium, Belize, Bermuda, Bolivia, Brazil, BVI, Canada, Cayman Islands, Chile, Colombia, Costa Rica, Dominica, Dominican Republic, Ecuador, El Salvador, France, Germany, Grenada, Guadeloupe, Guatemala, Haiti, Honduras, Italy, Jamaica, Japan, Martinique, Mexico, Netherlands Antilles, Nicaragua, Panama, Paraguay, Peru, Spain, St Kitts & Nevis, St Lucia, St Vincent & Grenadines, Sweden, Switzerland, Trinidad & Tobago, Turks & Caicos, United Kingdom, Uruguay and Venezuela.

American Airlines Fleet

Airbus A300-600R	35
Boeing 727-200	73
Boeing 737-800	18
Boeing 757-200	102
Boeing 767-200	8
Boeing 767-200ER	22
Boeing 767-300ER	49
Boeing 777-200IGW	11
Douglas DC-10-10	6
Douglas DC-10-30	5
Fokker F100	75
McDonnell-Douglas MD-11	11
McDonnell-Douglas MD-80	279
McDonnell-Douglas MD-90	5

FLEET TOTAL 699 (Average Fleet Age 10.7 years – correct to 1 September 1999)

Passengers Boarded	1999	84,747,000
	1998	81,424,000
	1997	80,700,000
	1996	79,300,000

Employees Systemwide 100,951

Chairman, President & CEO Donald J. Carty

Corporate Headquarters
4333 Amon Carter Blvd, Fort Worth, TX 76155, USA
Tel: +1 (817) 963 1234
Web site: http://www.aa.com

2) United Airlines
(Information correct to March 2000)

	Daily Departures		Airports Served
United Airlines	—	United Airlines	135
United Express	—	United Express	183
United Shuttle	468	United Shuttle	22
System Combined	2,330	System Combined (net of duplicates)	336

Daily Departures at Major Airports

City	Jet	Express	Shuttle	Total
Chicago O'Hare (Hub)	414	130	0	544
Denver (Hub)	247	195	31	473
San Francisco (Hub)	93	99	132	324
Los Angeles International (Hub)	98	179	105	382
Washington/Dulles International (Hub)	109	245	0	354

DESTINATIONS SERVED

Domestic
48 States in US, District of Columbia, 2 × US territories, Commonwealth of Puerto Rico.

International
Argentina, Australia, Belgium, Brazil, Canada, Chile, Costa Rica, El Salvador, France, Germany, Guatemala, Italy, Japan, Korea, Mexico, Netherlands, New Zealand, People's Republic of China (including Hong Kong), Peru, Philippines, Singapore, St Thomas, Taiwan, Thailand, United Kingdom, Uruguay, Venezuela.

United Airlines Fleet (Correct to January 2000)

Airbus A319	28
Airbus A320	55
Boeing 727-200	75
Boeing 737-200	24
Boeing 737-300	101
Boeing 737-500	57
Boeing 747-200	7
Boeing 747-400	43
Boeing 757-200	98
Boeing 767-200	19
Boeing 767-300	31
Boeing 777-200	39
Douglas DC-10-10	9
Douglas DC-10-30	3
Douglas DC-10-30F (freighter)	4

FLEET TOTAL 593 (Average Fleet Age 9.9 years – correct to January 2000)

Passengers Boarded	1999	87,160,000
	1998	87,000,000
	1997	84,400,000
	1996	81,860,000

Employees Systemwide 100,000

Chairman & CEO (UAL Corporation and United Airlines) James E. Goodwin

Corporate Headquarters
United Airlines, P.O. Box 66100, Chicago, IL 60666, USA
Tel: +1 (847) 700 4000
Web site: http://www.ual.com

3) Delta Air Lines
(Information correct to December 1999)

	Daily Departures		Airports Served
Delta Air Lines	2,440	Delta Airlines	158
Delta Connection	1,921	Delta Connection	170
Delta Express	162	Delta Express	21
Delta Shuttle	76	Delta Shuttle	3
System Combined	4,599	System Combined (net of duplicates)	235

Daily Departures at Major Airports

City	Jet	Connection	Express	Shuttle	Total
Atlanta Worldport (Hub)	662	240	0	0	902
Cincinnati/N. Kentucky International (Hub)	204	304	0	0	508
Dallas/Fort Worth (Hub)	123	64	0	0	187
Salt Lake City (Hub)	150	103	0	0	253
New York (JFK) (Hub)	50	59	0	0	109
Orlando	36	57	0	0	93

DESTINATIONS SERVED

Domestic
48 States in US (42 Jet, 48 including Delta Connection), District of Columbia, Commonwealth of Puerto Rico.

International
Belgium, Belize, Bolivia, Brazil, Chile, Colombia, Costa Rica, Ecuador, El Salvador, France, Germany, Guatemala, Honduras, Mexico, Nicaragua, Panama, Paraguay, Peru, Uruguay, Switzerland, United Kingdom, Venezuela.

Delta Air Lines Fleet

Boeing 727	131
Boeing 737-200	54
Boeing 737-347	15
Boeing 737-832	15
Boeing 757-232	91
Boeing 767-332	26
Boeing 767-332ER	33
Boeing 777-200	2
Lockheed L1011-1	23
Lockheed L1011-250	6
Lockheed L1011-500	16
McDonnell-Douglas MD-11	14
McDonnell-Douglas MD-88	120
McDonnell-Douglas MD-90	16

FLEET TOTAL — 562 (Average Fleet Age 13 years – correct to January 1998)

Passengers Boarded	1999	105,530,000
	1998	105,000,000
	1997	102,900,000
	1996	97,280,000

Employees Systemwide   65,000

President & CEO   Leo F. Mullin

Corporate Headquarters
Delta Air Lines, Inc., PO Box 20706, Atlanta, GA 30320, USA
Tel: +1 (404) 715 5876
Web site: http://www.delta-air.com/index.html

4) Northwest Airlines
(Information correct to October 1999)

	Daily Departures		Airports Served
Northwest Airlines	1,700	Northwest Airlines (US mainland)	155
Northwest Airlink	700	Northwest Airlink	78
System Combined	2,400	System Combined (US worldwide)	407

Daily Departures at Major Airports

City	NW Airlines	NW Airlink	Total
Minneapolis/St Paul (Hub)	372	153	525
Detroit (Hub)	380	148	528
Memphis (Hub)	175	101	276
Tokyo/Narita (Hub)	19	0	19
Osaka/Kansai (Hub)	7	0	7

DESTINATIONS SERVED

Domestic
46 States in US, District of Columbia, Commonwealth of Puerto Rico.

International
Trans-Atlantic Service – France (Paris), Germany (Frankfurt), India (Delhi and Mumbai), Netherlands (Amsterdam), UK (London)
Trans-Pacific Service – China (Beijing, Hong Kong, Shanghai), Indonesia (Jakarta), Japan (Nagoya, Osaka, Tokyo), Malaysia (Kuala Lumpur), Mariana Islands (Guam, Saipan), Philippines (Manila), Singapore, South Korea (Seoul), Taiwan (Taipei)
Trans-Border Service – Canada (Calgary, Edmonton, Montreal, Saskatoon, Toronto, Vancouver, Winnipeg), Mexico (Acapulco, Cancun, Cozumel, Ixtapa/Zihuatanejo, Los Cabos, Mexico City, Puerto Vallarta
Caribbean Service – British West Indies (Grand Cayman), Costa Rica/Liberia, Dominican Republic (Puerto Plata), Netherlands Antilles (St Maarten).

Northwest Airlines Fleet

Airbus A319	10
Airbus A320-200	70
Boeing 727-200 Advanced	31
Boeing 747-100	1
Boeing 747-200	19
Boeing 747-200F (freighter)	9
Boeing 747-400	14
Boeing 757-251	48
Douglas DC-9-10	10
Douglas DC-9-30	112
Douglas DC-9-40	12
Douglas DC-9-50	35
Douglas DC-10-30	20
Douglas DC-10-40	21
McDonnell-Douglas MD-82	8

FLEET TOTAL — 420 (Average Fleet Age 18 years – correct to October 1999)

Passengers Boarded	1999	56,114,000
	1998	50,500,000
	1997	54,720,000
	1996	52,700,000

Employees Systemwide   52,000

President & CEO   John H. Dasburg

Corporate Headquarters
Northwest Airlines, 5101 Northwest Drive, St Paul, MN 55111-3034, USA
Tel: +1 (612) 726 2331
Web site: http://www.nwa.com

5) US Airways

(Information correct to January 2000)

	Daily Departures		Airports Served
US Airways	1,841	US Airways	102
US Airways Express	2,546	US Airways Express	172
US Airways Shuttle	154	US Airways Shuttle	4
MetroJet	240	MetroJet	23
System Combined	4,781	System Combined	204

Daily Departures at Major Airports

City	Jet	Express	Shuttle	Total
Pittsburgh (Hub)	262	233	0	495
Charlotte, NC (Hub)	312	161	0	473
Philadelphia (Hub)	241	157	0	398
LaGuardia, New York	75	68	47	190
Boston	63	70	47	180
Ronald Reagan Washington (National)	78	65	30	173
Baltimore-Washington (Hub)	81	71	0	152
Washington-Dulles International	44	73	30	147
Tampa, Florida	39	45	0	84
Kansas City, Missouri	15	65	0	80
Orlando, Florida	50	21	0	71

DESTINATIONS SERVED

Domestic
38 States in US, District of Columbia, Commonwealth of Puerto Rico, US Virgin Islands.

International
Bahamas, Bermuda, Canada, Cayman Islands, France, Germany, Italy, Jamaica, Mexico, Netherlands Antilles, Spain and United Kingdom.

US Airways Fleet

Airbus A319	18
Airbus A320	8
Boeing 727-200	11
Boeing 737-200	64
Boeing 737-300	85
Boeing 737-400	54
Boeing 757	34
Boeing 767-200ER	12
Douglas DC-9-30	44
Fokker F100	40
McDonnell-Douglas MD-80	31
FLEET TOTAL	401

Passengers Boarded		
	1999	55,812,000
	1998	57,989,595
	1997	58,658,788
	1996	56,639,757
	1995	57,035,140
	1994	59,494,577
	1993	53,678,114
	1992	54,654,575
	1991	55,600,119

Employees Systemwide   43,028

Chairman   Stephen M. Wolf

President & CEO   Rakesh Gangwal

Corporate Headquarters
2345 Crystal Drive, Arlington, VA 22227, USA
Tel: +1 (703) 872 7000
Web site: http://www.usairways.com

6) Continental Airlines

(Information correct to January 2000)

	Daily Departures		Airports Served
Continental Airlines	1,372	Continental Airlines	125
Continental Express	884	Continental Express	*100
System Combined	2,256	System Combined (net of duplicates)	215

*(92 US / 8 international)

Daily Departures at Major Airports

City	Jet	Express	Total
Houston/George Bush Intercontinental (Hub)	350	172	522
New York/Newark (Hub)	269	115	384
Cleveland (Hub)	90	189	279
Boston	28	0	28
Atlanta	24	3	27
Ronald Reagan Washington National	24	1	25
Los Angeles	24	0	24
New Orleans	18	0	18
Guam	17	0	17

DESTINATIONS SERVED   (128 domestic and 69 international)

Domestic
42 States in US, District of Columbia, Commonwealth of Puerto Rico.

International
Atlantic/Caribbean – Antigua, Aruba, Bahamas, Bermuda, Dominican Republic, St Maarten
South America – Brazil, Chile, Colombia, Ecuador, Peru, Venezuela
Central America – Belize, Costa Rica, El Salvador, Guatemala, Honduras, Nicaragua, Panama
Europe/Mid East – Belgium, UK (England and Scotland), France, Germany, Ireland, Israel, Italy, Netherlands, Portugal, Spain, Switzerland
Micronesia – Guam and 10 other Pacific islands
S. Pacific/Far East – Australia, Hong Kong, Indonesia, Japan, New Caledonia, Philippines, Taiwan
North America – Canada, Mexico.

Continental Fleet

Boeing 727	22
Boeing 737	179
Boeing 757	36
Boeing 767 (on order and options)	47
Boeing 777	11
Douglas DC-9	11
Douglas DC-10	33
McDonnell-Douglas MD-80	69
FLEET TOTAL	361 (an additional 136 aircraft with Continental Express)

Passengers Boarded		
	1999	45,540,000
	1998	44,000,000
	1997	41,560,000
	1996	35,640,000

Employees Systemwide   49,300

Chairman & CEO   Gordon Bethune

Corporate Headquarters
1600 Smith Street, Houston, TX 77002, USA
Tel: +1 (713) 324 5000
Web site: www.flycontin